SHOW
- YOUR -
WORTH,
GIRL

Be Bold, Speak Up, and Be Heard
Teen Inspirations, Hints, Tips, and Truths

Dr. Marilou Ryder
Jessica Thompson

Show Your Worth, Girl

Copyright©2021 Marilou Ryder and Jessica Thompson

Paperback ISBN: 978-1-7356854-3-4

Kindle eBook: 978-1-7356854-4-1

Library of Congress Control Number: 2021938463

Printed in the United States of America
Delmar Publishing, Huntington Beach, CA 92648

SHOW
- YOUR -
WORTH,
GIRL

INTRODUCTION

To all the Young Teen Girls out there,

How is everything going? We hope all is well and you are thriving during your teen years. There is so much to manage and navigate right now. Sometimes it can be a good idea to have a plan and set some goals. We have written this small book, which we like to call an "Instagraphic", just for you and all your BFs. We hope you'll take away some uplifting ideas on building and developing your confidence, courage, and personal girl power.

We know it isn't easy being female in any decade. But you own this current generation, and we want you to succeed in ways you never thought possible. We want you to believe in yourselves. We encourage you to trust people that will support and mentor you throughout these years. Find strength in mentors who can coach, guide, and navigate you to make those hard choices and decisions. We know you are strong, spirited girls who have unlimited potential. Start by getting to know who you really are. Dig deep and attempt to find out what makes you unique. Find comfort and confidence in being different. What is it that you want right now, and what do you see yourself doing tomorrow?

We are so proud of you. We know that you are challenged every day by what life throws at you. Be strong, look up, and seize the moment. Now is the time to rise to the occasion and ***SHOW YOUR WORTH, GIRL!***

Shine on and believe in yourselves!

Sisters,
Marilou & Jess

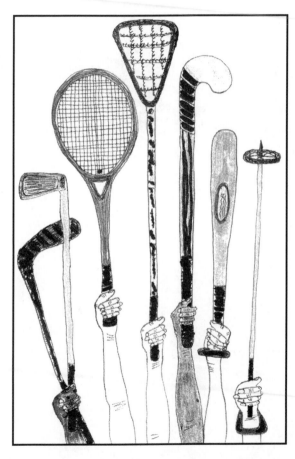

Girls are strong. So grab your sticks and play to win!

TAKE OUR 30 DAY CHALLENGE

**BE BOLD AND CONFIDENT
DR. MARILOU RYDER**

TRY A NEW STRATEGY EACH DAY

**WE CHALLENGE YOU
TO SHOW YOUR WORTH
JESSICA THOMPSON**

30 Day Challenges

#1. Thank one of your teachers for helping you

#2. Go four hours without using your cell phone

Tutorial
Women's History

Sarah Thomas became the first woman to officiate a Super Bowl in 2021.

Don't change so people will like you.

Emma

When I have friends over, my Mom says "Cool" all the time.

Well your Mom is sortta cool.

So you like her more than me?

That moment when you realize life begins at the end of your COMFORT ZONE

You start a new fundraiser to help a passionate cause.

You unplug tech gadgets for a No-Tech Sunday.

You speak to the School Board about an issue at school.

You get the courage to try a new activity.

You offer to tutor someone at your school who needs help.

You volunteer to start a new club in school.

You try out for the school play.

You take a chance and ask out that crush you like.

You spend a whole weekend with just your family members.

You challenge your teacher about a grade.

You run for school office or captain of your sport or club.

You apply to a college that you don't think you can get into.

#GIRLPOWERTIPS

Before you leave the
house each day, smile
in front of a mirror
as a great way to make
you feel happier and
more confident.

A lot of girls get mad at other girls over nothing and then exclude them from their next party, not speak to them again, or start a rumor about them. Most of us are afraid to confront someone that makes us angry. It's so easy to be direct and just say, 'You made me mad and you hurt my feelings'.

Emma

TODAY'S
Quote

Don't assume the worst when you see a crowd of people turn to look at you. They could be just thinking good things about you... like your jacket is cool.

LEAD. RUN. THINK. WORK. SPEAK UP. DREAM BIG.

LIKE A GIRL

Reminder

Rock the Boat

Okay

IT'S JUST A BAD DAY.

NOT A BAD
LIFE.

NOW PLAYING

Don't wait for an
opportunity, create it.

66

Being a teen girl is just plain confusing. Everyone tells you to be yourself but then they want you to look like Ariana Grande. (Alica)

Charlotte tried hard to help her grandmother understand
that she couldn't play Words With Friends all day long.

DON'T BE AFRAID TO SPEAK UP

BE BOLD ENOUGH TO BE HEARD

#GETYOURGIRLPOWER

confidence Booster

Think about a person you admire that seems really confident. Replicate one thing that person does throughout your day.

30 Day Challenges

#3. Volunteer at a local animal shelter

#4. Make dinner for your family

A friend is someone who does not make you feel insecure, left out, embarrassed, on edge or afraid.

FACTOID

ONE IN FIVE GIRLS AGES 12-18 ARE BULLIED 2-3 TIMES A MONTH OR MORE. **VERBAL HARASSMENT IS MOST COMMON (79%), FOLLOWED BY SOCIAL** HARASSMENT (50%), PHYSICAL **BULLYING (29%), AND CYBERBULLYING (25%).**[1]

#reachout

TODAY'S
Quote

Focus on all the good parts that make you amazing. You are a strong, smart, and worthy girl.

YES/ /NO

#I view critical feedback as a way to improve#

POP QUIZ

About 50% of all American children will witness the end of their parents' marriage.

☐ TRUE

☐ FALSE

TRUE: And teens with divorced parents are more likely to experience mental health problems requiring medication, counseling, or both. Girls with divorced parents are twice as likely to end up dropping out of high school than their peers who have parents who have not divorced. Seek out a caring adult or relative for help before things get too rough. *

*cited from https://legaljobs.io/blog/ children-of-divorce-statistics/

27

DON'T LET YESTERDAY

USE UP TOO
MUCH OF TODAY.

NOW PLAYING

Your only limit is your mind.

Head of the Table

In 1960 girls were taught how to set a table while the boys across the hall were taught how to make one. Today, you get to set the table, make the table, and sit at the head of the table.

WHO HAVE CONFIDENCE WILL RUN THE WORLD

Celebrate five decades of TITLE IX. We are
breaking barriers and kicking butt!

I KNOW
THAT I MAY
NOT BE GOOD
ENOUGH.
YET.

30 Day Challenges

#5. Avoid all packaged foods

#6. Teach a senior citizen a new tech move

Tutorial

Women's History

Lieutenant Madeline Swegle was the U.S. Navy's first African American female tactical fighter pilot in 2020.

Emma

My parents just told me not to throw shade on our plans for the holiday.

There should be a law against adults using slang.

No SH*T

#GIRLPOWERTIPS

Make a list of all the
things you are proud of.
Sometimes we focus so
much on what we are
not and overlook the
good stuff about us.

As a teen girl, it's really important to stand up for yourself. When was the last time you asked a coach or teacher about something you didn't understand or think was fair? Also, continue to ask for more responsibility as you get older. Advocate for yourself.

Sophia

TODAY'S
Quote

When someone gives
you a compliment,
no matter what,
learn how to say
"thank you".

SING. TRY HARD. BUILD. DELEGATE. CHALLENGE.

LIKE A GIRL

POP QUIZ

Girls avoid going to school when they feel bad about their looks.

☐ TRUE

☐ FALSE

TRUE: Over 70% of girls age 15-17 avoid normal daily activities, such as attending school, when they feel bad about their looks.* Take time today and compliment another girl.

*cited from http://www.ladiesofvalue.com/

Reminder

Know What's Real

Okay

STAND TALL

AND STAND OUT.

NOW PLAYING

Mistakes are proof you are trying.

"

I think the easiest thing to do when you're wrong is to admit you are and move on.
(Emma)

DON'T BE AFRAID TO BE SMART

WORK HARD TO CHANGE THE WORLD

#GETYOURGIRLPOWER

You can count on your friends to have your back.
But a few tips and truths from a friend that are
hard to take may help you become your best self.

confidence Booster

Eliminate all-or-nothing thinking from your life. For example, if you say, "I'm not good at math," or "I could never get an A in science," you immediately label yourself as a failure.

30 Day Challenges

#7. Offer to babysit a neighbor's child

#8. Donate clothes you haven't worn in six months

That moment when you realize the word COOL has no limits

You say 'No' when you feel uncomfortable in a situation.

You are usually the first one to raise your hand in class.

You are really good at math and science!

Your friends love your articles in the student newspaper.

You are a straight-A student.

You love posting inspirational messages.

You watch your weight but don't go overboard.

You belong to the drama and chess clubs and play in the marching band.

You are a size 16 and love how you look.

You don't need to be in a relationship to be happy.

You speak up for those being bullied.

You challenge authority with diplomacy.

#GIRLPOWERTIPS

Don't get caught up in
the drama of gossip.
Gossip can erode your
girl power.

BE BRILLIANT. BE SMART.
BE POSITIVE.
BE PRESIDENT.

LIKE A GIRL

TODAY'S
Quote

Perfect does not exist. But the words "pretty good" are a good stand-in.

YES/ /NO

#When things aren't going my way, I view it as a challenge#

Reminder

You are Worthy

Okay

SOMETIMES

YOU JUST HAVE TO LIVE

WITHOUT IT.

NOW PLAYING

Sometimes you win, sometimes you learn.

Slice of Life

There are two slices of pie left. One is slightly larger than the other. Do you take the smaller one or do you ask your friend to choose their slice first?

Girls

WHO PLAY SPORTS WILL LEAD THE WORLD

I KNOW THAT MY MISTAKES AND FAILURES DON'T DEFINE ME.

30 Day Challenges

#9. Go a whole day without spending any $$

#10. Get a library card and check out a book

After Libby's parents cancelled her phone apps,
she saw her future in Hologram technology.
No one would ever take her phone away again!

Tutorial

Women's History

Selena Gomez was the first person to reach 100 million followers on Instagram in 2016.

A friend is someone who does not talk badly about you to anyone.

FACTOID

TEENS WHO ARGUE WITH THEIR PARENTS ARE MORE LIKELY TO HAVE THE GUTS TO SAY "NO" TO FRIENDS, AND NOT CAVE TO PEER PRESSURE TO DO DRUGS, HAVE SEX, OR ENGAGE IN OTHER RISKY BEHAVIORS.[2]

#justsayno

Sometimes when I think about how to solve a problem or if I get angry with someone I decide that it's just not worth making a big deal out of it. I think it's better to change my attitude or keep my distance from a certain person. I have learned to pick my battles.

Amelia

TODAY'S
Quote

Be brave and take a
chance to leave your
safe comfort zone.
Take a risk to do
something new and
different.

YES/ /NO

#When I get together with my friends I try to avoid gossiping about other girls#

POP QUIZ

Girls are more afraid of becoming fat than they are of getting cancer or losing their parents.

☐ TRUE

☐ FALSE

TRUE: More than one in three girls who are actually a healthy weight try to diet. Teens who don't feel good about themselves are more likely to diet.* Increase your confidence by writing down a list of your past successes.

*cited from https://mrclhowe.weebly.com/uploads/5/5/0/4/55 041379/dieting_information_for_teens.pdf

22% of Mayors

11% of Astronauts

7% of Airline Pilots

13% of Engineers

ARE FEMALE

#dreambig

66

Almost every girl I know feels like they are not pretty enough, skinny enough, or smart enough. So many of my friends... all they think about is food. The pressures on teen girls to be more than 'just enough' are neverending.
(Madison)

IT'S A GOOD DAY TO MAKE A PLAN. WHAT WILL BE YOURS?

#GETYOURGIRLPOWER

confidence
Booster

Realize that no one has the
perfect life and everyone
has struggles. When you
think someone else's life
is better, happier, or easier
than yours, it can lower your
self-confidence.

30 Day Challenges

#11. Go a whole day without one complaint

#12. Learn how to change a flat tire

I wish I had her hair. I wish I had her eyes. I wish I had her smile. I wish I had her clothes. I wish the media would stop asking everyone, "Who wore it better?"

That moment when you know you need to get an ADULT in the room

You smell alcohol on your carpool driver's breath.

You don't have a plan for what to do after high school.

You think no one likes you at school.

You are seriously depressed.

You are worried about a girl at school getting bullied.

You need to offload some things on your plate.

Kids at school tell you to go back to where you came from.

Your parents are getting divorced and your world is turning upside down.

Your friends are mad and won't talk to you.

You believe you need to lose or gain more weight.

You think you could be LGBTQ.

You are failing two or more classes.

Never let
a boy be
mean to
you.

#GIRLPOWERTIPS

It takes guts to apologize. Saying, "I'm sorry" for something you've done means you know and respect yourself.

~~Social Media~~
^
fact checker

Try searching for the topic in an online fact-checker that can collect more than 100,000 fact checks from reputable publishers around the world.

TODAY'S
Quote

Sometimes you have to turn the corner to find a new beginning.

SHOW LOYALTY. SHOW PASSION. SHOW SPIRIT. SHOW UP.

LIKE A GIRL

POP QUIZ

Girls are not interested in pursuing STEM careers.

☐ TRUE

☐ FALSE

FALSE: Over 74% of high school girls are interested in the fields and subjects of STEM. Girls who like STEM are high achievers and have supportive adult networks.* Seek out a teacher if you want to know more about STEM fields.

*cited from https://www.uschamberfoundation.org/blog/post/ stem-engineering-future-women-science/42803

Reminder

You are not Alone

Okay

12% of Neurosurgeons

38% of Attorneys

8% of CFOs

28% of Stock Brokers

ARE FEMALE

#bebold

Comfort Food

You've seen a lot of historical firsts since you were born. There will be plenty more as you age. Surround yourself with people who will guide, support, and comfort you through the difficult ones.

PUT YOUR ENERGY WHERE YOUR HEART IS

#GETYOURGIRLPOWER

Ella is excited about her Sweet 16 Birthday party. All of her friends dread another Sweet 16 party but know it's good training for future bridesmaid's duty.

WHO TAKE
HEALTHY RISKS
ACTUALLY
INCREASE THEIR
CONFIDENCE
LEVELS

I KNOW THAT I CAN LOSE AND STILL HAVE FUN.

confidence Booster

If your parents say, "You'll never amount to anything," they may be speaking from anger or their own problems. Learn to understand where these messages come from and that they are not true. You are not worthless.

30 Day Challenges

#13. Practice filling out a job application

#14. Sit at a different lunch table

Tutorial
Women's History

Drew Gilpin Faust
became Harvard University's
first woman president in 2007.

FACTOID

TEEN GIRLS WORRY A LOT. HIGH SCHOOL HAS EVOLVED INTO A HIGH-STAKES LANDSCAPE. YOU WORRY THAT EVERY DECISION CAN HAVE AN IMPACT ON YOUR FUTURE. BUT YOU ALSO UNDERSTAND THAT THESE HIGH EXPECTATIONS, EXTENSIVE COMPETITION, AND LIMITATIONS MUST BE MANAGED. IT IS A CONSTANT BALANCING ACT. [3]

#youareincontrol

There's this really popular girl in school that everyone likes. One day she came over to me in the quad and said, 'You wear the coolest clothes.' I thanked her and now I say hi to her when I see her. She made me feel really special.

Mia

TODAY'S
Quote

You can talk about doing something all you want but nothing will happen until you make a plan. Get started now!

DEMAND. INVENT. ASSERT. COACH. HUG.

LIKE A GIRL

YES/ /NO

#I can cope when unexpected changes come into my life#

3% of Construction Workers

8% of Firefighters

12% of Police Officers

15% of City Managers

ARE FEMALE

#setyourgoalshigh

66

If you screw up, do what you can to set things right and then move on. (Olivia)

confidence
Booster

Make a habit of sending positive self-messages to yourself. The more positive messages you listen to and believe the more self-confident you will become.

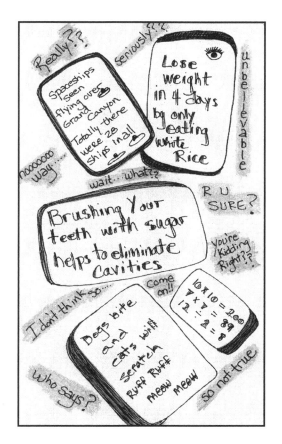

BREAKING NEWS! This Just In. Teenage boy reports that bugs with wings discovered around his house are actually flying bugs!

Emma

Mom, I just got the lead in the school play!

WTF

Mom, what do you think WTF means?

Well that's fantastic!

30 Day Challenges

#15. Take a walk without your phone

#16. Read an entire Wikipedia about a famous woman

#GIRLPOWERTIPS

Show your girl power
by sticking up for
someone being bullied.
You just may save
that person's life.

Don't talk. Just act.

TODAY'S
Quote

You only have one
body and one mind.
They are not replaceable
so treat them with
utmost respect.

POP QUIZ

More high school female grads enroll in college than males.

☐ TRUE

☐ FALSE

TRUE: Among high school graduates ages 16-24, the college enrollment rate for young women was 69.8% compared to 62% for young men.* Start researching college opportunities now.

*cited from https://www.bls.gov/news.release/hsgec.nr0.htm

Reminder

What's the Worst that Could Happen?

Okay

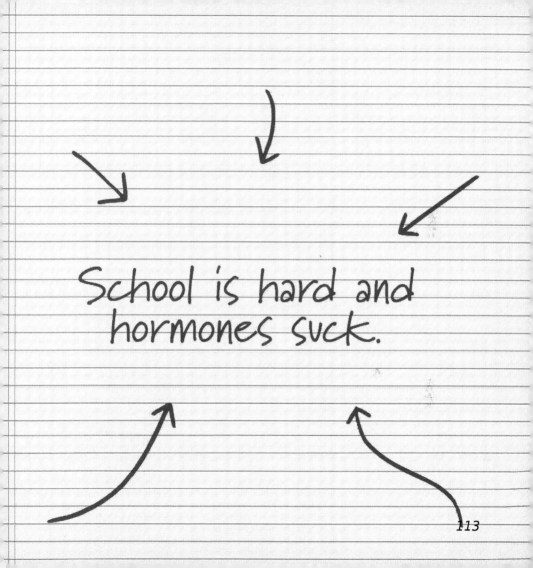

School is hard and
hormones suck.

CELEBRATE YOUR OWN WINS

THEN GO FORWARD
WITH THE NEXT
OPPORTUNITY

#GETYOURGIRLPOWER

Too much on your plate? Feeling stressed? Biting off more than you can chew? Oh wait, there's a support group for that called "Tortured Teens".

WHO LEARN TO CODE HAVE UNLIMITED OPPORTUNITY

30 Day Challenges

#17. Play a board game with a friend

#18. Donate your old toys to a homeless shelter

Tutorial

Women's History

Dr. Peggy Whitson became the first woman to command the International Space Station in 2008.

Social ~~Media~~
^
fact checker

Check to see if a news
item has more than one source
by Googling to find out if
it can be found on other
news channels.

FACTOID

TEENS ARE CONSIDERED "ADULTS" AT AGE 18. YET, MRI SCANS SHOW THAT THE PARTS OF THE **BRAIN INVOLVED IN DECISION-MAKING** DON'T BECOME FULLY DEVELOPED UNTIL AGE 25.[4]

#foodforthought

I can honestly say it is a common occurrence for others in a group to make fun of others. I'm pretty sure we do this to make ourselves feel better than that person. A few times I have said, 'Who knows what they are going through?' which stops the conversation for a while.

Alex

YES/ /NO

#When negative thoughts come into my head I don't let them throw me into a tailspin#

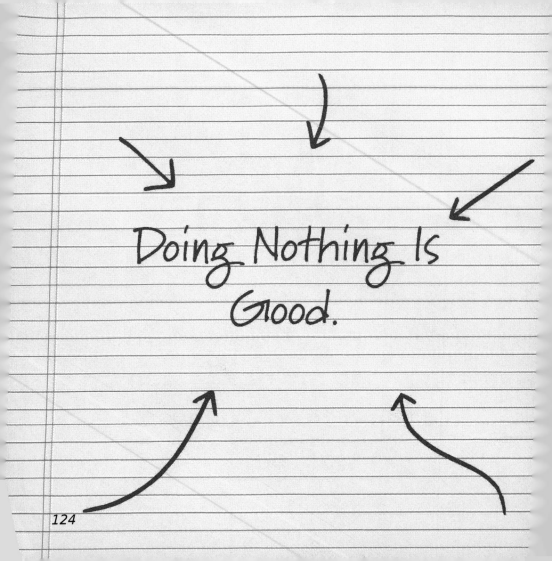

Doing Nothing Is
Good.

124

66

> *Losing with grace and humility will someday take you to the championship.*
> **(Haley)**

Choosy Girl

Make friends with the people you like, not the ones you think you should be friends with.

Class, who can share one fact about the male species?

30 Day Challenges

#19. Tell your BF what you like about him or her the best

#20. Eliminate the words "I can't" from your mind

That moment when you realize you are beginning to find your VOICE

You limit self-deprecating talk.

You ask questions when you don't understand something.

You never say, "I'm just a girl."

You tune into your intuition.

Your friends and adults ask, "What do YOU think?"

You don't ask for permission to speak.

You believe you are worthy.

You have learned to silence that little voice in your head that says you're stupid.

You advocate for others.

You attribute your successes to skill rather than chance.

You are not afraid to speak up about important issues.

You want to be seen for who you really are.

#GIRLPOWERTIPS

Avoid using speech
patterns that limit
your girl power like,
"This may sound stupid..."
or "I know I may have
this all wrong."

A friend is someone who does not act one way to you when you're alone together and then completely different in front of other people.

Let me know when you arrive at Megan's.

Do you need anything?

Did you bring food?

Do you have your sweater?

Say hi to Megan's mom for me.

Mom, I just arrived at Megan's house.

TODAY'S
Quote

Take the lead when you can. There will be plenty of times when you have to follow.

WEAR A UNIFORM. MARCH. BE FIRST. BE STRONG.

LIKE A GIRL

POP QUIZ

The majority of girls end up marrying their first boyfriend.

☐ *TRUE*

☐ *FALSE*

FALSE: Only 2% of marriages are from a high school relationship and only 25% of women say they married their first love.* Keep all your options open.

*cited from https://mensdivorce.com/high-school-sweethearts/

Temperature Check

 I embrace the moment

 I tell my family I love them

 I believe my potential is unlimited

WHO MESS UP AND THEN RECOVER BOOST THEIR OWN CONFIDENCE

I KNOW THAT OTHER PEOPLE ARE BETTER THAN ME AT SOME THINGS.

**confidence
Booster**

Make a list of all the things
you are grateful for. When
you focus on the good in
your life you strengthen your
positive thinking. Gratitude
thinking builds confidence.

FACTOID

MELATONIN, THE HORMONE THAT MAKES YOU SLEEPY, IS **RELEASED LATER AT NIGHT IN A TEEN'S** BRAIN AND HANGS AROUND **FOR LONGER** THE NEXT DAY. THAT'S WHY YOU DON'T FEEL SLEEPY UNTIL AFTER 10 PM AND CAN BE GROGGY IN THE MORNING.[5]

#beauty&brainsleep

Emma

I hate it when adults say 'you kids sit on your phone all day and don't do any real socializing'.

Yeah, how'd that work out for them during the Pandemic?

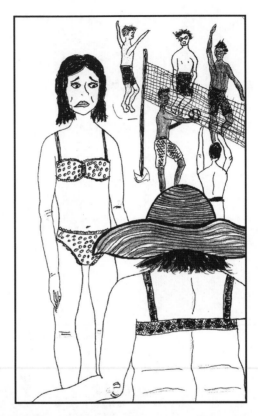

Emily loved that 73-year-old Aunt Bella had the courage to wear a thong on the beach. But now Emily needed to summon her own courage to tell Aunt Bella that her thong was on backwards.

I try really hard to listen to people when I'm in a group, you know, remember their name, what their hobby is, that sort of thing. When I see the person again and call them by their name they seem surprised and happy. I feel like I know the whole school by their first name and I think it makes a difference in how I am treated.

Alicia

It's okay to ask for help. How do you think all those successful women got to where they are today?

YES/ /NO

#When a girl walks into the room my immediate response is to compliment rather than judge her#

POP QUIZ

The average age for a woman to get married is 18.

☐ TRUE

☐ FALSE

FALSE: The average age for heterosexual women to marry is 35.7. By comparison, the average age for same-sex couples is 36.6 for women.* Take time to find your one and only soul mate.

*cited from https://www.theguardian.com/uknews/2020/apr/14/average-age-for-heterosexualmarriage-hits-35-for-women-and-38-for-men

Reminder

Skip the Drama

Okay

Temperature Check

 I stay connected to my playful side

 I am curious

 I say 'I can' rather than 'what if'

> **So many of my friends have major FOMO over not being in a relationship. Yes, high school is more fun if you are in a relationship but my advice is to take your time to be in a good one.**
> **(Ava)**

Point of View

Consider extracurricular activities that encourage working in a team. Collaborative action will help you learn to communicate with others who have different points of view.

HANG OUT WITH GIRLS

WHO EMBRACE THE

COMPETITIVE

SPIRIT

#GETYOURGIRLPOWER

30 Day Challenges

#21. Post an inspiring quote on social media

#22. Ask a successful woman how she got there

Tutorial
Women's History

Gina Haspel became the first woman Director of the Central Intelligence Agency in 2018.

#GIRLPOWERTIPS

When someone tells
you "No" find a way
to advocate for yourself
by providing supportive
reasons to back up
your idea.

Don't promise. Just prove.

Emma

My parents just took away my Snapchat and Instagram accounts.

Ugh, you poor thing. That's not fun.

Now they have no one to follow on social media.

157

30 Day Challenges

#23. Google the phrase gender stereotypes

#24. Research a career typically pursued by males

TODAY'S
Quote

Don't be afraid to challenge authority. If you do it with confidence and grace you will be respected.

GET ELECTED. TAKE CHARGE. SOLVE PROBLEMS. JUST DO IT.

LIKE A GIRL

Temperature Check

 My friends like to be around me

 I can reframe a negative thought

 I can make myself laugh

Girls

WHO DON'T FEEL PRESSURED TO BE PERFECT ARE ON THEIR WAY TO UNLIMITED **SUCCESS**

I KNOW THAT I
DON'T HAVE
TO BE
PERFECT.
I CAN BE GOOD
ENOUGH.

I dream about...

Tutorial
Women's History

Kathryn Bigelow was the first woman to win
the Academy Award for Best Director for
The Hurt Locker in 2010.

Social ~~Media~~
^ fact checker

Search an image by touching and holding the image on your phone which will look for the photo to see if it has appeared online before. You will be able see if it has been altered from its original meaning.

FACTOID

TEEN GIRLS WORRY A LOT ABOUT HOW THEY CAN **IMPROVE, AND** OFTEN SET UNREALISTIC EXPECTATIONS FOR THEMSELVES **THAT ARE DIFFICULT** TO MEET. MANY GIRLS FEEL RELENTLESS PRESSURE **TO BE THE BEST.**[6]

#setgoalsyoucanmeet

Emma

My parents say I should start volunteering.

Oh yeah? Where?

Here at home. Ugh.

30 Day Challenges

#25. Go a whole day without comparing yourself to others

#26. Join a cause to change the world

That moment when you realize you might love your PHONE more than you think

You own more phone cases than shoes.

Your phone answers all your questions making you an automatic genius.

You kiss your phone after dropping it.

You purchase a phone sanitizing machine.

You can kiss your boyfriend and text at the same time.

You drop your phone into a porta-potty and fish it out.

You check your phone again to see what time it is because the first time you weren't paying attention.

Your phone has its own pillow in bed.

You tap your pocket and panic when you can't feel your phone.

You can't post a selfie without using a filter app.

You say you're going to bed but really mean you are texting your BFs.

You give your phone a name.

#GIRLPOWERTIPS

When you learn that you didn't qualify for something you really wanted, summon your inner girl power and ask, "What are my next steps?"

When my parents got divorced I was so confused and anxious. At first, I was relieved because all they ever did was fight. Then all I cared about was where would I live, what about school and my friends? Once I talked about my feelings, I learned I wasn't alone. So many of my friends felt the same way when their parents divorced.

Tamara

YES/ /NO

#I have a backup plan in case my goals are not met#

POP QUIZ

A majority of teenage girls want to be their own boss when they grow up.

☐ *TRUE*

☐ *FALSE*

TRUE: According to recent studies, nearly 8 in 10 girls in grades 5-12 say they want to be their own boss. Over 45% of girls say they plan to start their own business and 42% say they will invent something that will change the world.*

*cited from https://www.wholekidsfoundation.org /blog/new-young-entrepreneurs-pilot-grant

Em·pow·er·ment

/em   pourment/

1: becoming stronger and more confident, especially in controlling one's life and claiming one's rights.

2: you, hopefully

"

A lot of times when you feel depressed people will tell you to "get over it" or "just stop being depressed." Take it from me, depression is serious. Tell a close teacher, school counselor or parent that you need to talk to someone.

(Madeline)

In It to Win It

Girls need to know how to play the game and how to play to win even if losing. Make "good" competition a part of your healthy mindset.

DON'T WISH FOR IT

WORK FOR IT!

#GETYOURGIRLPOWER

Him: "You run like a girl."

Her: "Run a little faster and you can too, Joe."

A friend is someone who does not make you feel as if you must compete for their attention or approval.

Emma

Every time my mom and I take a photo together she makes a duck face.

Mine too. Pathetic

30 Day Challenges

#27. Eat a food you've never tried before

#28. Close your eyes and listen to your surroundings

TODAY'S
Quote

Divorce doesn't happen to teenagers it happens to their parents. Unfortunately, you have to deal with the changes and it isn't fun. Strap in and get ready for the ride. Hang on, stay strong, know you are loved, safe, and never alone. With time the ride will end and you will know just where you belong.

LOVE. FORGIVE. BE GENEROUS. BE WISE.

LIKE A GIRL

POP QUIZ

Girls brought up in a negative environment have low self-esteem.

☐ TRUE

☐ FALSE

FALSE: Everyone can find some reason not to have healthy self-esteem. No matter what your childhood experiences were, self-esteem comes from what you think about yourself. How you think about yourself is your choice.*

*cited from https://www.theguardian.com/uknews/2020/apr/14/ average-age-for-heterosexualmarriage-hits-35-for-women-and-38-for-men

Con·fi·dent

[kon-fi-dent]

1: a person who believes in oneself and abilities

2: you, hopefully

I KNOW
I CAN ACCEPT
THINGS I
CANNOT
CONTROL.

Don't tell me. Show me.

FACTOID

WHILE ONLY 6% OF FORTUNE 500 CEOS ARE WOMEN, 90% OF THEM PLAYED SPORTS IN HIGH SCHOOL AND 54% PLAYED SPORTS AT THE UNIVERSITY LEVEL. [7]

#participationpoints

Emma

My teachers are always telling us to be good to our parents.

What do you think they mean?

Maybe take them shopping? IDK

#GIRLPOWERTIPS

Choose to compete in something- board games, sports, just anything. The contest is not imortant but learning to compete is critical for lifelong success.

Self-ad·vo·ca·cy

/self-advakse/

1: learning how to speak up for yourself, making your own decisions about your life

2: you, hopefully

I am 17 and personally, I would rather be called a 'girl' over being called a 'woman'. And if someone calls me a 'lady' I think it's a term for a woman who sits up straight and crosses her legs.
(Addison)

30 Day Challenges

#29. Be the first to raise your hand in class

#30. Ask an adult for their opinion on something

We Hope You Enjoyed Our Book

SPEAK UP	RAISE YOUR HAND	SMILE A LOT	STAND UP TALL	THINK POSITIVE
LOOK UP	START SOMETHING NEW	TRY NOT TO BE PERFECT	KNOW YOU CAN	TAKE A CHANCE
TURN THE PAGE	MAKE SOMEONE HAPPY	:)	LOSE WITH GRACE	LAUGH AT YOURSELF
VOLUNTEER	BE BRILLIANT	ENTER THE RACE	RISE ABOVE IT	TAKE THE LEAD
SIT IN THE FRONT ROW	BE GOOD TO YOURSELF	STOP A BULLY	CHALLENGE AUTHORITY	SHOW YOUR WORTH

REFERENCES

Bonior, A. (2011). *The Friendship Fix*. St. Martin's, New York.

Carnegie, D. (2005). *How to Win Friends and Influence People for Teen Girls*. Simon & Schuster, New York.

Ottaviano, P. (2015). *Girl World*. Source Books, Illinois.

Porges, M. (2020) *What Girls Need*. Viking, New York.

Schab, L. (2017). *The Self-Esteem Habit for Teens*. New Harbinger Publication, California

NOTES

1. Youth Truth. *Learning from Student Voice: Bullying* (2020). Retrieved from https://youthtruthsurvey.org/bullying/

2. Hanrahanyouth. January 2020 Newsletter. Retrieved from. https://www.hanrahanyouth.com/single-post

3. Carter, C. (2020). *High School Worries: 5 Things High School Girls Worry About Most*. Retrieved from https://yourteenmag.com/health/teenager-mental-health/high-school-girls-worry

4. Dutton (2014). *Maturity Doesn't Happen at 18*. Retrieved from https://cafemom.com/parenting/180339-scientific_facts_about_teens_teenagers/124031-theyre_better_at_making_friends

5. Cleare, A. (2020) *Weird and Wonderful Facts about Teenagers*. Retrieved from https://anitacleare.co.uk/weird-wonderful-facts-teenagers/

6. Carter, C. (2020). *High School Worries: 5 Things High School Girls Worry About Most*. Retrieved from https://yourteenmag.com/health/teenager-mental-health/high-school-girls-worry

7. Orr, E. (2020). *Forget the Score, Just Play*. Retrieved from https://www.kornferry.com/insights/briefings-magazine/issue-33/forget-the-score-just-play

Books from our Sister to Sister Series

www.sistertosistersecrets.com

Don't Forget Your Lipstick, Girl

SISTER to SISTER SECRETS
for Gaining
CONFIDENCE, COURAGE, and POWER

DR. MARILOU RYDER
JESSICA THOMPSON

DR. MARILOU RYDER
JESSICA THOMPSON

Don't Forget Your Sweater, Girl

SISTER to SISTER SECRETS
for AGING with
PURPOSE and HUMOR

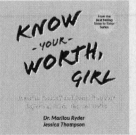

KNOW -YOUR- WORTH, GIRL

Dr. Marilou Ryder
Jessica Thompson

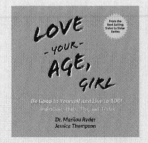

LOVE -YOUR- AGE, GIRL

Dr. Marilou Ryder
Jessica Thompson

Made in the USA
Las Vegas, NV
18 November 2022

59638115R00111